Tiger's Illustrated Dictionary

English – Somali

Editors

Aruna Shah

Sushil Sharma

Design & Illustration

Mrinal Mitra

Tiger's Illustrated Dictionary: English – Somali

Published by: Tiger Books Ltd.
18 Thirlmere Ave.
Perivale. Middx
UB6 8EF
(UK)

First Edition: 2004

ISBN: 0 948137 63 0

Introduction

This visually stimulating dictionary tells a story on each page in a unique way. The colourful illustrations will familiarize children with words based on subjects they are curious to learn about. The topics such as Beach, Circus, and Zoo will attract young readers' attention and entice them to browse through the pages many a time. The subjects and words are carefully chosen to enhance vocabulary in English and the home language selected in the bi-lingual edition.

Children will enjoy looking at the main pictures and linking them with associated word-grid on opposite pages. It will help them develop reference skills in an enjoyable way.

In bi-lingual editions, each word-grid contains an original English word with translation in language script, followed by its transliteration in roman script. This will be useful for parents and children both in understanding words and their meanings in English and the home language as well as cross-referencing between them. The index section only includes original English word and transliteration of the language word in roman script, which will help teachers and others to understand and pronounce words from another language.

Every effort has been made to keep the dictionary as close to "nature" as possible and familiarize children with environment and animal kingdom they find so fascinating.

Central to all main illustrations is a little tiger cub, who appears to enjoy his world of travel and adventures as he journeys through various subjects. Children will grow fond of him and will be attracted to embark on his letterland journey. In that way, the book goes beyond the realms of just an illustrated dictionary and assumes something of a picture storybook!

The bi-lingual, dual-text dictionary will be a very useful learning resource in multicultural environment.

PASSPORT CONTROL

Aeroplane Diyaarad	Arrival Imaansho	Departure Dhoofid	Gangway Suqduud
Hangar Hooso	Luggage Boorso	Passenger Rakaab	Passport Bassaboor
Pilot Duuliye	Radar Raadeer	Runway Garoon	Trolley Tarooli

Bucket Baaldi	Crab Carsaanyo	Hawker Xaraashle	Pebbles Qaruurax
Pier Macmal	Sand Castle Qalacad Ciideed	Seagull Xuur	Seaweed Dhirbadeed
Shell Qolof	Spade Badeel	Swimmer Dabaalyahan	Towel Tuwaal

B
B
B

Acrobat Qalaamarogad	Band Koox	Carousel Badhad	Clown Majaajilayste
Dog Eey	Elephant Maroodi	Horse Faras	Juggler Riixe
Magician Sixiroole	Tent Teendho	Trapeze Bir	Unicycle Baskeel lugle

Cactus Tiintiin	Camel Geel	Caravan Rimoor	Hawk Dafo
Lizard Bulac	Mirage Dhalanteed	Oasis Naq	Ostrich Goronyo
Palm Tree Geed Qumbe	Sand Dunes Cii	Scorpion Dabaqalooc	Snake Mas

E Earthquake

Dhulgarir

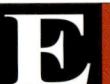

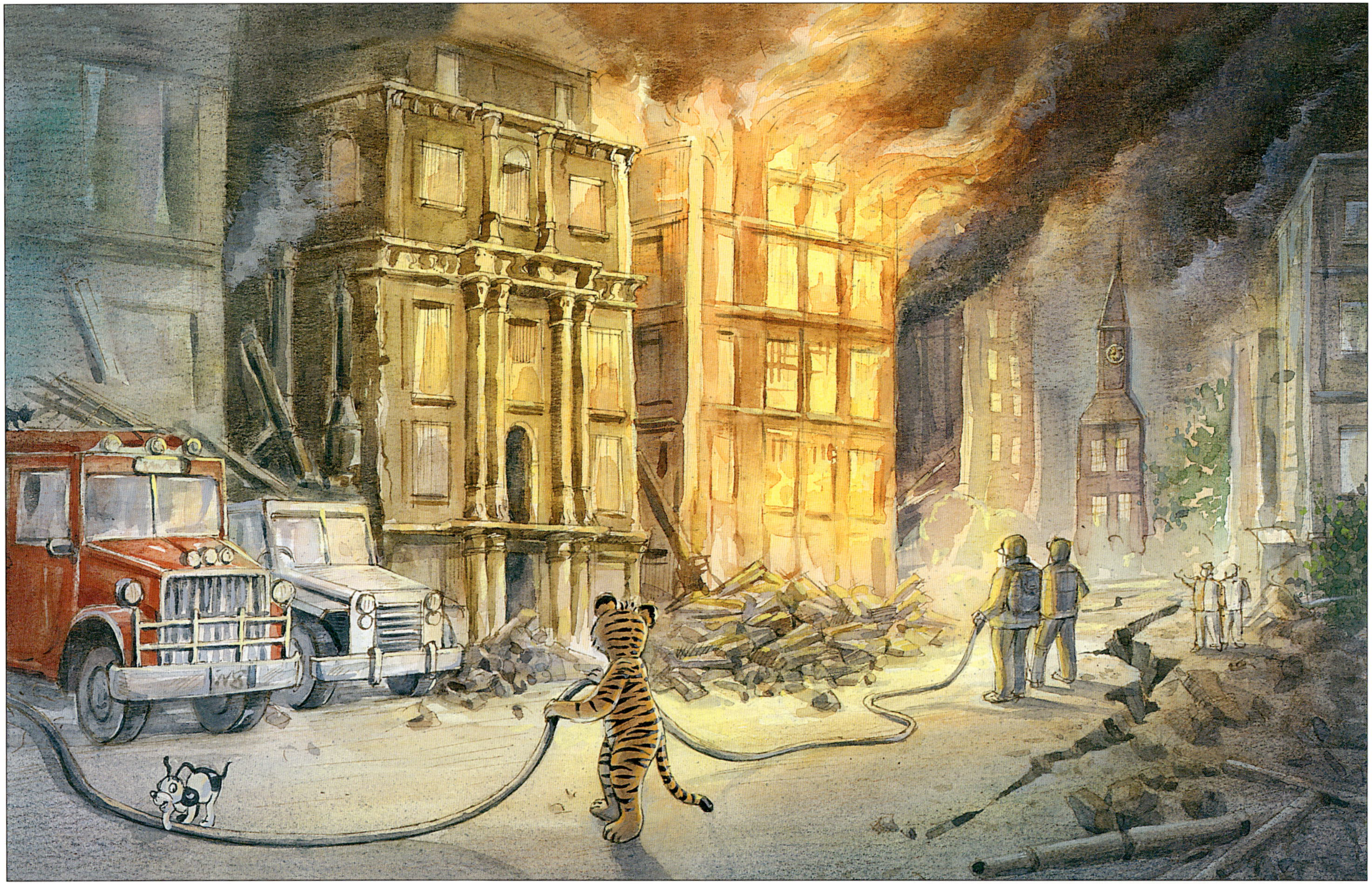

Ash Dambas	Crack Dilaac	Crater Bohol	Eruption Qarax
Fire Dab	Geyser Biyo Kulul	Grit Milix	Lava Laafa
Rock Dhadhaab	Seismograph Sisimogaraf	Smoke Qiiq	Volcano Dabdhul

11

Apple Tufaax	Apricot Abrikoot	Banana Moos	Cherry Jeeri
Grapes Cinab	Mango Canbe	Melon Qare	Orange Liin
Pear Canbaarud	Pineapple Cananaas	Plum Blaam	Strawberry Istarooberi

13

Bushes Duur	Fence Deyr	Flower Ubax	Fountain Biyo Duul
Gardener Jardiinyeeri	Hose Pipe Dooni Guri	Lawn Ardaag	Plant Abuur
Sparrow Qooleey	Squirrel Dabagaale	Watering Can Tanag	Wheelbarrow Gaar Gacan

Basil Reexaan	Bay Leaf Caleen	Chives Jaafis	Coriander Kabsar Caleen
Dill Dhill	Fennel Fenel	Mint Nacnac	Oregano Sactar
Parsley Kamsar	Rosemary Tusbax	Sage Saaji	Thyme Thyme

Ant Quraanjo	Beetle Geesoole	Bumble Bee Faxal	Butterfly Balanbaalis
Cricket Jiiq - Jiiqle	Firefly Gaarabidhan	Grasshopper Ayax	Honey Bee Shini
Ladybird Caasha Qurun	Moth Geedo Gable	Spider Carro	Wasp Laxle

Bamboo Baambuu	Bear Madax Kuti	Deer Deero	Jackal Dawac
Leopard Shabeel	Monkey Daanyeer	Parrot Buqbuqaani	Tiger Shabeel
Tree Geed	Vine Geed Cinab	Wolf Uubato	Woodpecker Wuudhpecker

21

Balloon Buufin	Candy Macmacaan	Chocolate Shukulaato	Drinks Cabitaano
Ice Cream Jalaato	Newspaper Wargays	Paper Warqad	Pen Qalin
Pencil Qalin Qori	Sharpener Qalin Qor	Souvenir Macduun	Toys Tareen

Boat Doon	Cabin Qol	Crocodile Yaxaas	Fish Kaluun
Fisherman Kalunumeyste	Flamingo Xuur Badeed	Heron Qayaquuto	Hippopotamus Jeer
Pelican Belikaan	Reed Dooga Bihaya	Stork Istork	Swan Iswaan

Avalanche Afalaanj	**Glacier** Baraf Qulqula	**Mist** Dhedo	**Mountain Goat** Ari Buureed
Mountaineer Buurfuule	**Slope** Dhaadhac	**Snow** Baraf	**Snow Leopard** Shabeel Baraf
Stream Qulqulid	**Summit** Dusha Sre	**Valley** Dooxo	**Waterfall** Biyo Dhac

Bat Fiidmeer	**Bed** Sariir	**Candle** Shumac	**Darkness** Gudcur
Dream Riyo	**Lamp** Nal	**Lantern** Faynuus	**Moonlight** Caddo
Owl Guumeys	**Sleep** Hurdo	**Sleeping Bag** Baga hurdada	**Star** Xidig

Coral Shacabi	Diver Quusaa	Dolphin Hoombaro	Lighthouse Musawac
Octopus Sanaani	Penguin Binguwin	Puffin Bufin	Sea-lion Libaax Badeed
Ship Markab	Turtle Qubbo	Wave Hir	Whale Nibiri

32

Bench Foom	Duck Boolo Boolo	Gate Albaab	Grass Doog
Kite Aabiteey	Park Keeper Xadiiqad Ilaaliye	Picnic Dalxiis	Pond Bali
Sandpit Hog	Slide Siibasho	Swing Weecasho	Water Lily Dhir Biyood

Carriage Gaari Faras	Castle Qalcad	Court Maxkamad	Crown Taaj
Guard Wardiye	Jewels Jowharad	King Boqor	Palace Qasri
Procession Socod	Sceptre Usha Boqorka	Throne Kursiga Boqorka	Tiara Taaj

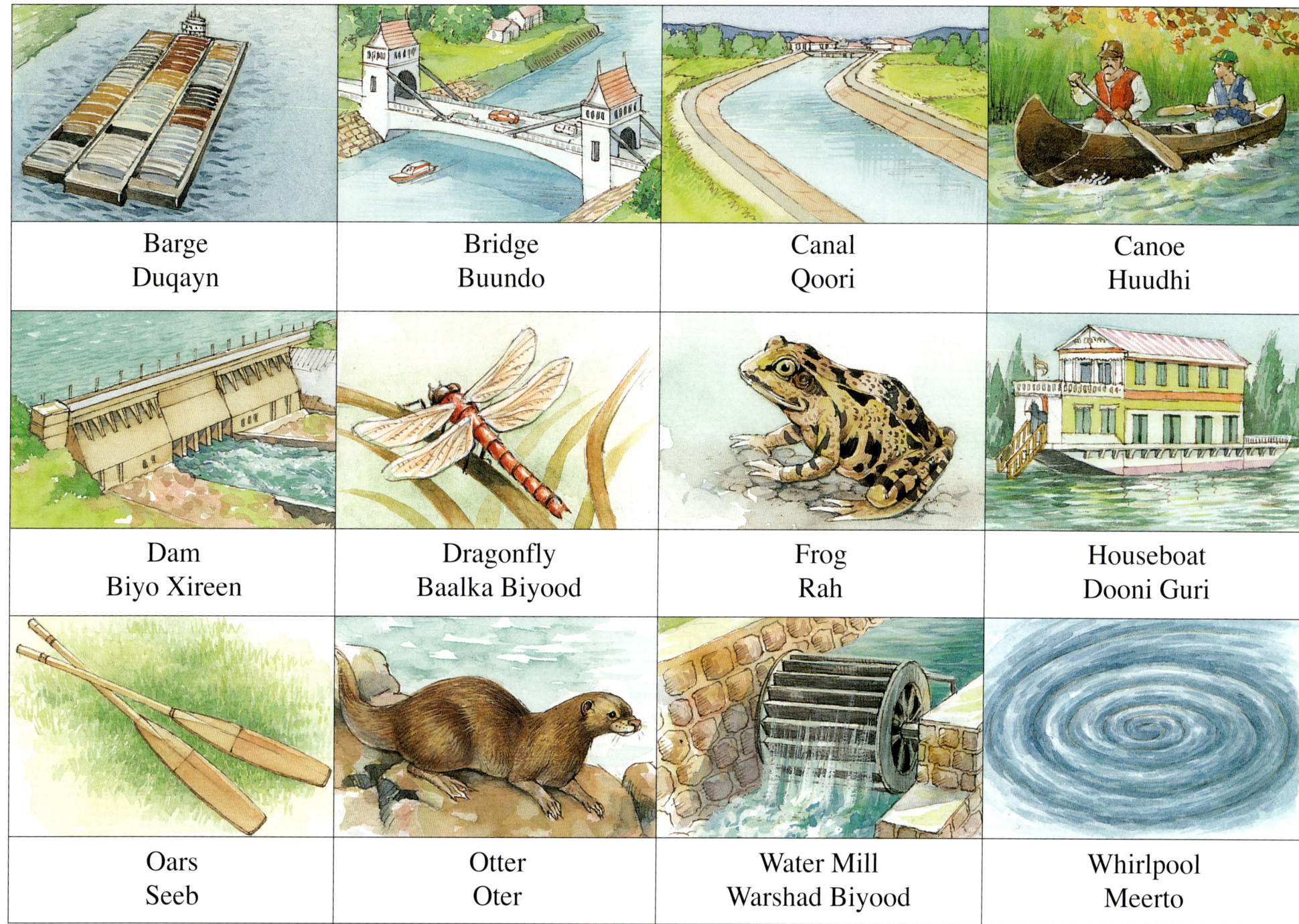

Barge Duqayn	**Bridge** Buundo	**Canal** Qoori	**Canoe** Huudhi
Dam Biyo Xireen	**Dragonfly** Baalka Biyood	**Frog** Rah	**Houseboat** Dooni Guri
Oars Seeb	**Otter** Oter	**Water Mill** Warshad Biyood	**Whirlpool** Meerto

Badminton Baadhminton	Basketball Kubadda kolayga	Cricket Kiriket	Football Kubadda Cagta
Golf Goolaf	Hockey Xeego	Judo Lagdin	Karate Kaaratee
Polo Bolo	Rugby Ragbi	Tennis Teenis	Wrestling Musaaraco

Bicycle Baaskiil	Bus Bas	Car Baaburr	Ferry Feeri
Helicopter Diyaarad	Hovercraft Hooferkaraft	Motorbike Mooto	Sledge Baabuur Baraf
Taxi Tagsi	Train Tareen	Tram Taraam	Truck Gaari Xamuul

Earth Dhul	Jupiter Jubitar	Mars Maars	Mercury Meerkuri
Moon Dayax	Neptune Nibtuun	Planets Meerayaal	Pluto Baluuto
Saturn Satun	Sun Qorax	Uranus Yuraynus	Venus Vinus

Beans Digir	Brinjal Birinjaal	Cabbage Kaabaj	Carrot Dabacase
Cauliflower Koolifiyoore	Mushroom Baraabuf	Onion Basal	Peas Dhamancaso
Potatoes Baradho	Pumpkin Bocor	Radish Bagal	Tomato Tamaandho

Blizzard Dabay Baraf	**Cyclone** Leexo	**Flood** Daad	**Fog** Ceeryaamo
Frost Dhaxan	**Hurricane** Gufaaco	**Ice** Baraf	**Lightning** Biriq
Rain Roob	**Storm** Duufaan	**Sunny** Cadceed	**Tornado** Uffo

 Castanets Kaastaneto	 Cymbal Biyati	 Drum Reeme	 Flute Faloot
 Gong Goongo	 Horn Gees	 Oboe Oobiyo	 Rattle Jabaq
 Sitar Sitar	 Tambourine Shambal	 Trumpet Turunbo	 Violin Dhexyar

Binocular Doorbin	Capstan Bir Duubto	Compass Jiheeye	Dinghy Shaximaad
Harbour Dekad	Knot Gutin	Lifebuoy Layfboy	Marina Furdad
Rope Xarig	Sail Laash	Sea Bad	Skipper Kabtan

Alligator Yaxaas	Cheetah Harancass	Chimpanzee Daanyeer	Giraffe Geri
Kangaroo Kangaruu	Lion Libaax	Panda Baando	Peacock Daaíuus
Python Jebisco	Rhinoceros Wiyil	Tortoise Diin	Zebra Dameer Farow

53

Index

Acrobat	Qalaamarogad	7
Aeroplane	Diyaarad	3
Airport	Gegi	2
Alligator	Yaxaas	53
Ant	Quraanjo	19
Apple	Tufaax	13
Apricot	Abrikoot	13
Arrival	Imaansho	3
Ash	Dambas	11
Avalanche	Afalaanj	27
Badminton	Baadhminton	39
Balloon	Buufin	23
Bamboo	Baambuu	21
Banana	Moos	13
Band	Koox	7
Barge	Duqayn	37
Basil	Reexaan	17
Basketball	Kubadda kolayga	39
Bat	Fiidmeer	29
Bay Leaf	Caleen	17
Beach	Xeeb	4
Beans	Digir	45
Bear	Madax Kuti	21
Bed	Sariir	29
Beetle	Geesoole	19
Bench	Foom	33
Bicycle	Baaskiil	41
Binocular	Doorbin	51
Blizzard	Dabay Baraf	47
Boat	Doon	25
Bridge	Buundo	37
Brinjal	Birinjaal	45
Bucket	Baaldi	5
Bumble Bee	Faxal	19
Bus	Bas	41
Bushes	Duur	15
Butterfly	Balanbaalis	19
Cabbage	Kaabaj	45
Cabin	Qol	25
Cactus	Tiintiin	9
Camel	Geel	9
Canal	Qoori	37
Candle	Shumac	29
Candy	Macmacaan	23

Canoe	Huudhi	37
Capstan	Bir Duubto	51
Car	Baaburr	41
Caravan	Rimoor	9
Carousel	Badhad	7
Carriage	Gaari Faras	35
Carrot	Dabacase	45
Castanets	Kaastaneto	49
Castle	Qalcad	35
Cauliflower	Koolifiyoore	45
Cheetah	Harancass	53
Cherry	Jeeri	13
Chimpanzee	Daanyeer	53
Chives	Jaafis	17
Chocolate	Shukulaato	23
Circus	Bandhig	6
Clown	Majaajilayste	7
Compass	Jiheeye	51
Coral	Shacabi	31
Coriander	Kabsar Caleen	17
Court	Maxkamad	35
Crab	Carsaanyo	5
Crack	Dilaac	11
Crater	Bohol	11
Cricket	kiriket	39
Cricket	Jiiq - Jiiqle	19
Crocodile	Yaxass	25
Crown	Taaj	35
Cyclone	Leexo	47
Cymbal	Biyati	49
Dam	Biyo Xireen	37
Darkness	Gudcur	29
Deer	Deero	21
Departure	Dhoofid	3
Desert	Saxaare	8
Dill	Dhill	17
Dinghy	Shaximaad	51
Diver	Quusaa	31
Dog	Eey	7
Dolphin	Hoombaro	31
Dragonfly	Baalka Biyood	37
Dream	Riyo	29
Drinks	Cabitaano	23
Drum	Reeme	49

Duck	Boolo Boolo	33
Earth	Dhul	43
Earthquake	Dhulgarir	10
Elephant	Maroodi	7
Eruption	Qarax	11
Fence	Deyr	15
Fennel	Fenel	17
Ferry	Feeri	41
Fire	Dab	11
Firefly	Gaarabidhan	19
Fish	Kaluun	25
Fisherman	Kalunumeyste	25
Flamingo	Xuur Badeed	25
Flood	Daad	47
Flower	Ubax	15
Flute	Faloot	49
Fog	Ceeryaamo	47
Football	Kubadda Cagta	39
Fountain	Biyo Duul	15
Frog	Rah	37
Frost	Dhaxan	47
Fruit	Khudrad	12
Gangway	Suqduud	3
Garden	Jardiino	14
Gardener	Jardiinyeeri	15
Gate	Albaab	33
Geyser	Biyo Kulul	11
Giraffe	Geri	53
Glacier	Baraf Qulqula	27
Golf	Goolaf	39
Gong	Goongo	49
Grapes	Cinab	13
Grass	Doog	33
Grasshopper	Ayax	19
Grit	Milix	11
Guard	Wardiye	35
Hangar	Hooso	3
Harbour	Dekad	51
Hawk	Dafo	9
Hawker	Xaraashle	5
Helicopter	Diyaarad	41
Herbs	Qayaquto	16
Heron	Qayaquto	25
Hippopotamus	Jeer	25

Hockey	Xeego	39
Honey Bee	Shini	19
Horn	Gees	49
Horse	Faras	7
Hose Pipe	Dooni Guri	15
Houseboat	Dooni Guri	37
Hovercraft	Hooferkaraft	41
Hurricane	Gufaaco	47
Ice	Baraf	47
Ice Cream	Jalaato	23
Insects	Cayayaano	18
Jackal	Dawac	21
Jewels	Jowharad	35
Judo	Lagdin	39
Juggler	Riixe	7
Jungle	Kayn	20
Jupiter	Jubitar	43
Kangaroo	Kangaruu	53
Karate	kaaratee	39
King	Boqor	35
Kiosk	Goodhi	22
Kite	Aabiteey	33
Knot	Gutin	51
Ladybird	Caasha Qurun	19
Lake	Haro	24
Lamp	Nal	29
Lantern	Faynuus	29
Lava	Laafa	11
Lawn	Ardaag	15
Leopard	Shabeel	21
Lifebuoy	Layfboy	51
Lighthouse	Musawac	31
Lightning	Biriq	47
Lion	Libaax	53
Lizard	Bulac	9
Luggage	Boorso	3
Magician	Sixiroole	7
Mango	Canbe	13
Marina	Furdad	51
Mars	Maars	43
Melon	Qare	13
Mercury	Meerkuri	43
Mint	Nacnac	17
Mirage	Dhalanteed	9

Mist	Dhedo	27
Monkey	Daanyeer	21
Moon	Dayax	43
Moonlight	Caddo	29
Moth	Geedo Gable	19
Motorbike	Mooto	41
Mountain	Burr	26
Mountain Goat	Ari Buureed	27
Mountaineer	Buurfuule	27
Mushroom	Baraabuf	45
Neptune	Nibtuun	43
Newspaper	Wargays	23
Night	Habeen	28
Ocean	Bad	37
Oars	Seeb	9
Oasis	Naq	49
Oboe	Oobiyo	30
Octopus	Sanaani	31
Onion	Basal	45
Orange	Liin	13
Oregano	Sactar	17
Ostrich	Goronyo	9
Otter	Oter	37
Owl	Guumeys	29
Palace	Qasri	35
Palm Tree	Geed Qumbe	9
Panda	Baando	53
Paper	Warqad	23
Park	Xadiiqad	32
Park keeper	Xadiiqad Ilaaliye	33
Parrot	Buqbuqaani	21
Parsley	Kamsar	17
Passenger	Rakaab	3
Passport	Bassaboor	3
Peacock	Daaíuus	53
Pear	Canbaarud	13
Peas	Dhamancaso	45
Pebbles	Qaruurax	5
Pelican	Belikaan	25
Pen	Qalin	23
Pencil	Qalin Qori	23
Penguin	Binguwin	31
Picnic	Dalxiis	33
Pier	Macmal	5
Pilot	Duuliye	3
Pineapple	Cananaas	13
Planets	Meerayaal	43
Plant	Abuur	15
Plum	Blaam	13
Pluto	Baluuto	43
Polo	Bolo	39
Pond	Bali	33
Potatoes	Baradho	45
Procession	Socod	35
Puffin	Bufin	31
Pumpkin	Bocor	45
Python	Jebisco	53
Queen	Boqorad	34
Radar	Raadeer	3
Radish	Bagal	45
Rain	Roob	47
Rattle	Jabaq	49
Reed	Dooga Bihaya	25
Rhinoceros	Wiyil	53
River	Webi	36
Rock	Dhadhaab	11
Rope	Xarig	51
Rosemary	Tusbax	17
Rugby	Ragbi	39
Runway	Garoon	3
Sage	Saaji	17
Sail	Laash	51
Sand Castle	Qalacad Ciideed	5
Sand Dune	Cii	9
Sandpit	Hog	33
Saturn	Satun	43
Sceptre	Usha Boqorka	35
Scorpion	Dabaqalooc	9
Sea	Bad	51
Seagull	Xuur	5
Sea-lion	Libaax Badeed	31
Seaweed	Dhir Badeed	5
Seismograph	Sisimogaraf	11
Sharpener	Qalin Qor	23
Shell	Qolof	5
Ship	Markab	31
Sitar	Sitar	49
Skipper	Kabtan	51
Sledge	Baabuur Baraf	41
Sleep	Hurdo	29
Sleeping Bag	Baga hurdada	29
Slide	Siibasho	33
Slope	Dhaadhac	27
Smoke	Qiiq	11
Snake	Mas	9
Snow	Baraf	27
Snow Leopard	Shabeel Baraf	27
Souvenir	Macduun	23
Spade	Badeel	5
Sparrow	Qooleey	15
Spider	Carro	19
Sports	Ciyaaro	38
Squirrel	Dabagaale	15
Star	Xidig	29
Stork	Istork	25
Storm	Duufaan	47
Strawberry	Istarooberi	13
Stream	Qulqulid	27
Summit	Dusha Sre	27
Sun	Qorax	43
Sunny	Cadceed	47
Swan	Iswaan	25
Swimmer	Dabaalyahan	5
Swing	Weecasho	33
Tambourine	Shambal	49
Taxi	Tagsi	41
Tennis	Teenis	39
Tent	Teendho	7
Throne	Kursiga Boqorka	35
Thyme	Thyme	17
Tiara	Taaj	35
Tiger	Shabeel	21
Tomato	Tamaandho	45
Tornado	Uffo	47
Tortoise	Diin	53
Towel	Tuwaal	5
Toys	Tareen	23
Train	Tareen	41
Tram	Taraam	41
Transport	Gaadiid	40
Trapeze	Bir	7
Tree	Geed	21
Trolley	Tarooli	3
Truck	Gaari Xamuul	41
Trumpet	Turunbo	49
Turtle	Qubbo	31
Unicycle	Baskeel lugle	7
Universe	Dunida	42
Uranus	Yuraynus	43
Valley	Dooxo	27
Vegetables	Khudrado	44
Venus	Vinus	43
Vine	Geed Cinab	21
Violin	Dhexyar	49
Volcano	Dabdhul	11
Wasp	Laxle	19
Waterfall	Biyo Dhac	27
Water Lily	Dhir Biyood	33
Water Mill	Warshad Biyood	37
Watering Can	Tanag	15
Wave	Hir	31
Weather	Jawi	46
Whale	Nibiri	31
Wheelbarrow	Gaar Gacan	15
Whirlpool	Meerto	37
Wolf	Uubato	21
Woodpecker	Wuudhpecker	21
Wrestling	Musaaraco	39
Xylophone	Saylafon	48
Yacht	Doon Yar	50
Zebra	Dameer Farow	53
Zoo	Zuu	52

INDEX